HEART FROM ANOTHER ERA

PAGES FROM MY HEART

AKSHAT RAWAT

Made with ♥ on the Notion Press Platform
www.notionpress.com

Contents

Contents

Preface

Hey! This is the collection of my experiences that has been shaped in the form of poems. In the pages that follow, you will encounter a collection of poetry that delves into the depths of my teenage years. This anthology, titled "Heart from Another Era," is a reflection of my inner world during a time of significant growth and change. Each poem is a piece of my journey, capturing the emotions and insights that defined my adolescence.

Welcome to "Heart from Another Era," a deeply personal collection of poetry that represents the essence of my teenage years. This anthology is a tapestry of my emotions, thoughts, and experiences during this transformative period of my life. Each poem serves as a window into my soul, offering a glimpse into the myriad feelings and perspectives that have shaped me.

In this collection, I have woven together diverse opinions and viewpoints, capturing the complexity of adolescence. My hope is that through these poems, you will not only connect with my journey but also find reflections of your own teenage years. Whether you are currently navigating this tumultuous time or reminiscing about your past, I believe these verses will resonate with you.

"Heart from Another Era" is more than just a compilation of poems; it is an invitation to introspection and empathy. Through my words, may you find a sense of kinship and a deeper understanding of the universal experiences that bind us all.

Acknowledgements

I would like to extend my heartfelt gratitude to my friend, Aryan Sharma, for his invaluable assistance in editing and reviewing this book. His meticulous efforts and insightful feedback have been indispensable. His unwavering support and dedication have significantly enhanced the quality of this work, and for that, I am deeply appreciative.

I would also like to thank my family and other friends for their continuous support and encouragement throughout this journey. Your belief in me has been a constant source of motivation.

I'm but a frame

"This poem is written from the unique perspective of someone who has passed away. The poem reflects on the narrator's life, recalling moments of joy and gratitude. Despite no longer being alive, the narrator finds solace in remembering the positive impact that certain people had on their life. This sense of gratitude allows the narrator to experience happiness even in death, as they cherish the memories of their living days."

.

.

1. Poetry

I'm but a frame.

As i go whispering down a forgotten street,
As I go wandering where shadows meet,
You always visit me in my grief,
Until I'm buried beneath autumn's leaves.
.

As I live, there's no one here
To claim me their, to hold me near.
But you, you dare, to stake your claim,
Though I'm cursed with a heart so deep,
A soul so pure, yet a fate so steep.
.

You come to hold me, to call my name,
In the daylight hours when . I'm but a frame.
When I am unconscious, you cry and weep,
Until my body's in the fire, your love you keep.
.

You call my soul, you adore,
In every whisper, you say once more,
As always, I hear your heartfelt plea,
"I love you a lot," eternally.

The Day You Will Become a Man

"The Day You Become a Man" holds a profound significance in my life, as it encapsulates the heartfelt message my father shared with me when I questioned his dedication to serving our nation. It embodies the wisdom and sacrifice he imparted, emphasizing the virtues of bravery, duty, and integrity. Through this poignant poem, I carry forward his legacy and the enduring bond between father and son."

2. Poetry

The Day You Will Become a Man

My son, the day you become a man,
You'll understand the reasons why,
I always urged you to be brave and strong,
Without needing to glorify

.

That day, you'll see why I couldn't stay,
Beside you in our village, for duty called me away.
As a man's worth isn't in what he can hold,
But in the values and virtues that make him bold.

.

A man embraces others with love and plays his part,
In this vast world, be a gentle heart.
He grasps the essence of duty and fate,
A man does what he must, despite the weight.

.

Of obstacles and pressures, it's never too late,
To live with integrity and affect others' state.
Value lies not in wealth, nor noble birth,
But in the legacy you leave on this earth.

.

You'll understand why I had to serve,
And complete the noblest plan,
To guard our forests, our rivers, our land.
For a true man's heart is where his duties stand,
And this, my son, you'll one day understand.

Childhood

"This poem unveils my journey, echoing the complexities of my ongoing teenage years. It delves into the depths of my emotions and the struggle between inner reality and outward appearance. May this poem resonate with you, offering insight into the ongoing quest for understanding and self-discovery."

.

.

.

.

.

.

.

"Children often know two worlds: the familiar home and the strange outside. Yet, some remain as if they've known only one world , of strangers." --- Akshat rawat

3. Poetry

Childhood

For others, tomorrow is always full of hope,
But for me, it's always a slippery slope.
Others' passion and talent are always appreciated,
As their families have them, all they needed.

.

But my talent never had a chance to come and spring,
Besides appreciation, only taunts and scorn I bring.
While others feel joy at a very high tone,
The resonance of my heart is still unknown.

.

When they fall ill, they have someone to take care,
But I always find pain, sorrow, and vacant air.
When they play with joy and wave at me, "hi";
My heart doesn't reply, as it only knows to say goodbye.

.

When they talk about love and friendship,
they find me gone,
As old I loved; I loved alone.
When they talk about feelings that they comb,
I only know about sadness which brings me home.

.

When I tell them about the sadness that I hold,
They say the answer to my love may remain untold.
But the question is, I never dare to love, so how can it be gone?
All they taught me is to pret, to understand their dusk and dawn.

.

When others convey their feelings with a shining tone and tear,
My heart, without emotions, remains sincere.
Now, I always keep a smile on my face,
But my heart remains without dignity and grace.

.

Now I don't blame God for not giving me care,
But still, I wait to know how it feels when someone hugs you and calls you "theirs."
In the evening of no moon and misty mess,
I wonder if it happens, is it just hormones, then,
Why am I not bless?

.

Why is this world not as it seems?
First, it gives me hope,
And then vanishes all my dreams.
For others, tomorrow always gleams,
But why does sadness and sadness in my p.o.v, it seems.

Feelings Can't Be Compared

"This poem delves into the complexity of human emotions, highlighting the inability to truly understand another's feelings despite our attempts at sympathy. It emphasizes the poignant nature of expression and open embrace in alleviating burdens. Yet, amidst this, it underscores the ineffable nature of feelings, forever beyond comparison."

"Despite our earnest efforts, we remain bound by the limits of our own perceptions, unable to fully grasp the depth of another's experience. Sympathy may bridge the gap, yet the true essence of another's pain or joy eludes our comprehension." --- Akshat rawat

4. Poetry

Feelings Can't Be Compared

Feelings are things which could never be compared,
Whether joy, pain, sorrow, or frightened fear.
The best and most beautiful things, they say,
Are felt with the heart, where true treasures lay.

.

Emotions that shatter can also mend,
The one that breaks your heart can sometimes be friend.
In risking it all, we find profound grace,
The only way to happiness is an open embrace.

.

Bravery is loving with no strings to tie,
Unconditionally, like the boundless sky.
We can't stop the waves that life brings our way,
Yet we choose which emotions to ride and display.

.

In the depths where our souls seek,
Promise are the language of feelings, profound and unique
When the essence of life's true meaning is share,
But feelings remain beyond compare.

Falling Towards Purpose

This poem captures life as a fall, drawing parallels between falling and life's journey. It emphasizes the inevitability of death and encourages embracing each moment, letting go of burdens, and finding purpose. The fall is not just an end, but a chance to rise, discover, and fulfill one's divine role.

·

·

·

·

·

·

·

·

·

. "You cannot give to people what they are incapable of receiving."

- This quote is attributed to *Agatha Christie*.

5. Poetry

Falling towards purpose

Life is like a plummet from a cliff to the ground,
No past to cling to, no retreat to be found.
At birth, deastiny's death is sealed,
And as we fall, fate's bed is revealed.

.

So Instead of waiting for death's call,
Or pointing fingers at God's wall,
Savor each moment, let joy unfurl,
For this journey is not eternal.

.

Weak branches won't hold; let them go,
They only cause suffering, don't you know?
If our end is death or a rough landing sound,
Discover your role before all this unbound.

.

Let your soul confess to God, truth and lies,
For God nudges you from cliffs, not to fall, but to rise.
In kindness, God recalls us before soul hit the ground,
But find your purpose before the next round.

.

Sacrifice pride, lust, greed, and selfish deeds,
Even yourself, if for greater good needs.
For in this way, if you sacrifice,
In golden book you won't die

.

As God calls you before the ground's embrace,
He'll let you see, with Him, your own race.
When you find God on His divine throne,
He offers you what you truly own,

The moon is beautiful isn't it

"This poem is a philosophical exploration crafted through the lenses of multiple thinkers, each contributing to convey the bittersweet essence of love. It navigates the paradoxical nature of desire and the transient beauty of existence, drawing upon the wisdom of various philosophical perspectives. What insights did you glean from this poetic journey through the complexities of love?"

6. Poetry

The moon is beautiful, isn't it?

In the heavens aglow with stars so highs,
If the moon i claim mine; longing increase as it flies.
But if I have it, it lose it's hype

.

I prefer to lose it beside being too wise.
Though it always in Mercurial guise
bittersweet love tail as it in lies

.

Its shifting forms, though unseen
higher handedness definitely has been
In love's gaze, pain's depth it does keen.
last massage "the moon is beautiful isn't it?" remains unseen.

What does a human seek

Ever wondered what people really seek in life? This poem dives into that quest for meaning, showing how we search far and wide for peace and truth. It reveals that true fulfillment isn't found in wealth or fame, but within our own souls, highlighting that the real challenge lies within our minds.

"And the day came when the risk to remain tight in a bud was more painful than the risk it took to blossom.""---Anaïs Nin

7. Poetry

What does a human seek

What does a human seek, in the vast expanse of sky?

To leave behind all they have, and bid the world goodbye.

Those who are In search of peace, they roam afar, through valleys deep and wide bazar,

Those who are already in peace leave to find some sapphire and haar

Yet find it not in golden halls, nor treasures, by their side.

.

For what they truly yearn, lies not in wealth or in fame

But in the quiet of the soul, where they never seek to claim

To shed the weight of worldly woe, and let the spirit to soar,

To find the truth that's always been, breathing in their heart and core, .

.

So let them search, let them seek, wheather through hell's depth and heaven's peak ,

Until they find the light within, that guides them through the tenebrae thread. .

For in the end, when all is said,

The real uphill lies within their head.

Unheard & Untold

"This poem delves into our unheard stories and unseen burdens,
echoing the weight we all carry silently within ourselves."

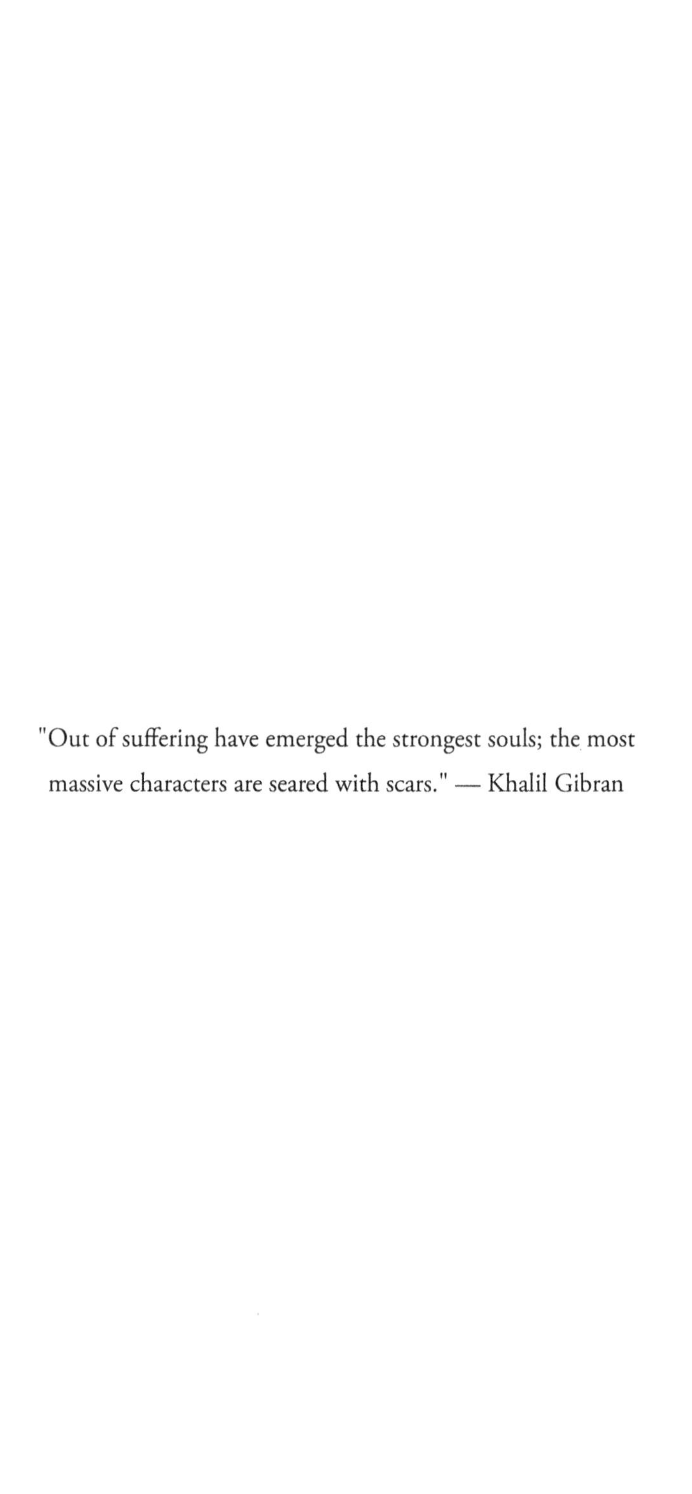

"Out of suffering have emerged the strongest souls; the most massive characters are seared with scars." — Khalil Gibran

8. Poetry

Unheard & Untold

Hate's grip tightens with each unwanted recall,
A weapon? A monster? A child, standing tall.

.

Once innocent eyes, now carry time's weight,
In a world where childhood rushed, at an alarming rate.

.

Expected as heroes, in shadows we roam,
Raised by cold eyes, taught not to bemoan.

.

We all hold stories, locked tight in our chest,
Chapters untold, where our secrets rest.

.

Just because I carry it so well,
Doesn't mean it's not heavy to tell.

.

Just like Atlas, I hold with grace,
Beside the burden which I embrace.

Universe in Your Eyes

"This poem captures love's essence, finding a universe in someone. The last paragraph speaks truth: those who drown in love see their beloved uniquely, embodying unparalleled beauty. Yet, this perspective is subjective; others may not see the same. "

"So for some a smile, for some a frown."

9. Poetry

Universe in Your Eyes

Amidst the chaos of life's grand design,

I stumbled upon you, unexpected, divine,

A poem in motion,

A universe in your eyes.

.

If beauty lies in the eyes, then you're the limit I portray,

Your eyes are like a garden where beautiful brown cosmos display.

Your presence is like a song, a poem,

Which steals all my words away.

.

I could compare you

To a thousand different things,

Yet words falter, unable to capture

The depth of my love, and the trance it brings.

.

You are my because in every why,

The answer to questions unasked,

The museum full of art;

I only have eyes for you.

.

I fell for you, and I'm still falling,
Through every high and every low.
The most beautiful part is,
I wasn't even looking when I found you.

.

So show me your thorns, your pain, your fears,
I'll hold you close, wipe away your tears.
For in your vulnerability, I found my home in you
With hands ready to bleed, love anew.

.

My darling, you will never be unloved by me,
Too well tangled in my soul;
Too deeply rooted to every part.
I carry you always, in every beat of my heart.

.

As sea speaks truth to those who'd drown,
So for some a smile, for some a frown.

Walking towards

"This poignant poem delves into the depths of fear and self-doubt, portraying how mental pressure can shape one's perception of themselves. It reflects on the internal struggle of questioning one's actions and identity amidst darkness and uncertainty."

.

.

.

.

.

.

.

.

.

"Deep into that darkness peering, long I stood there, wondering,
fearing, doubting, dreaming dreams no mortal ever dared to
dream before." — Edgar Allan Poe

10. Poetry

Walking towards

Am I walking towards something I should be running away from?
Is it a shadow, a will, or me but in a different form?
Is it really making me happy, joyful, or inadequately forlorn?
.

Is this street dark from the beginning, or is it darkened now on?
Is this whisper a song or a demonic chanting drawn?
Why do people say it's a curse to feel something unknown?
.

Is this giving me company or cover from dusk till dawn,
Or making me a phantom in the absence of me, and move on?
Is it common to feel the presence of someone who is none but dust?
.

Is it good when, in the most terrifying moments, your fear doesn't bust?
Is it okay to see souls and develop for them a lust?
Am I really walking towards something

"I should be running away from?"

The soldiers of aid

"This poetry is written to honor the sacrifice that soldiers make for us. It depicts their courage and bravery, although it only scratches the surface of the immense sacrifices they truly make for our safety and freedom."

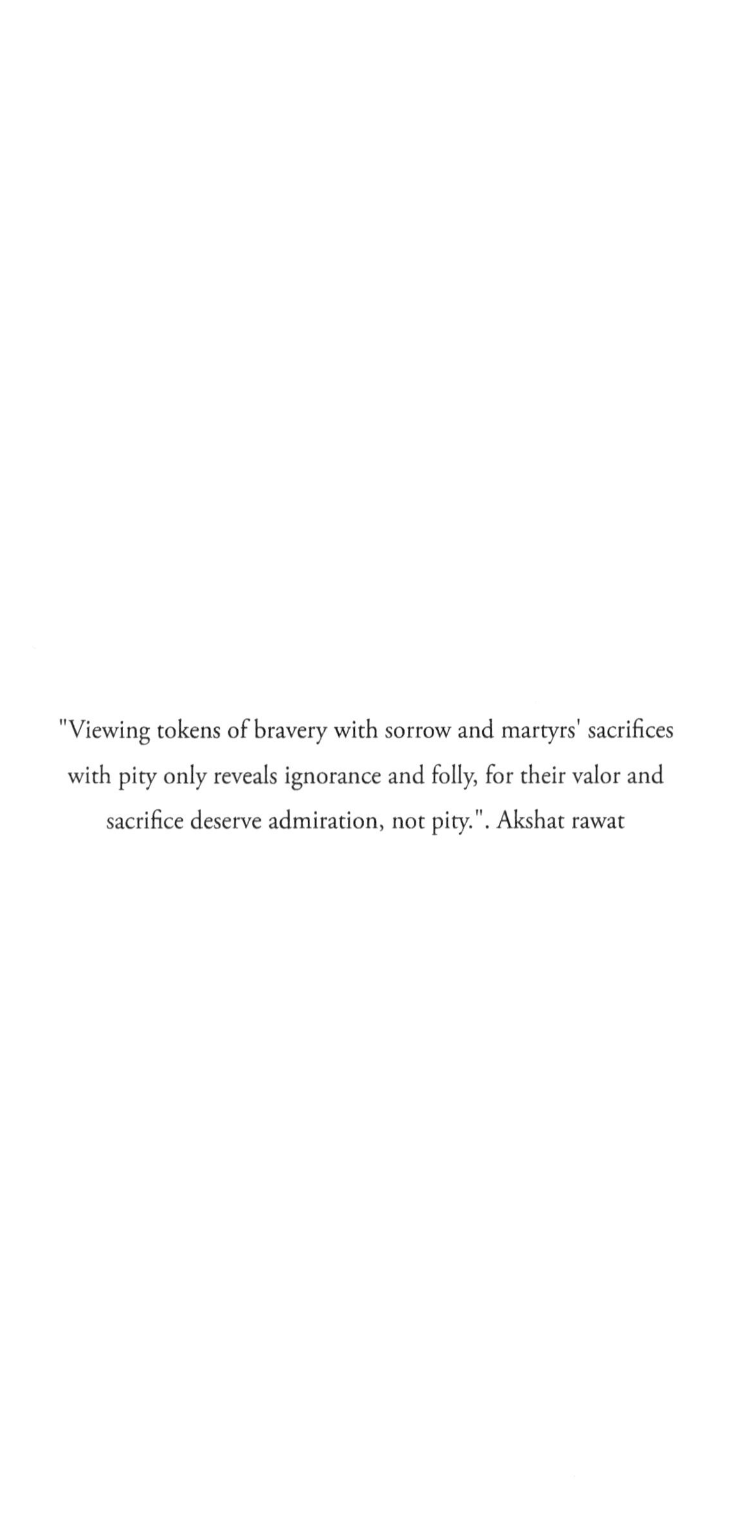

"Viewing tokens of bravery with sorrow and martyrs' sacrifices with pity only reveals ignorance and folly, for their valor and sacrifice deserve admiration, not pity.". Akshat rawat

11. Poetry

The soldiers of aid

.In fields of courage, a soldier stands tall,
With valor and honor, answering the call.
Through battles fought and sacrifices made,
A guardian of freedom, undying aid.

.

Battles fought, with valor and might,
Defending the innocent, in darkness and light,
Through tears and fears, unwavering they stay,
Their sacrifice, an oath they faithfully portray.

.

In lands far from home, their courage takes flight,
A beacon of hope in the midst of the fight,
With hearts full of duty, and courage, they sail,
Through storms of adversity, they never fail.

.

Leaving loved ones, they answer the call,
Their selflessness, the greatest gift for all,
Saluting those who gave their all,
For those who may them never recall.

.

And as the sun sets on battles well fought,

Their legacy lives on, a lesson well taught,

For in their sacrifice, we should find the way,

To honor their courage, each and every day.

.

..... Jai hind ....

Has this year started without me ?

"This poem conveys the haunting perspective of a person who, unbeknownst to them, lives a year after their passing. It delves into the agony of rejection and misunderstanding faced upon discovering their own demise. Through raw emotion and vivid imagery, witness the surreal journey of a soul navigating the agony of the afterlife."

.

.

.

.

.

.

.

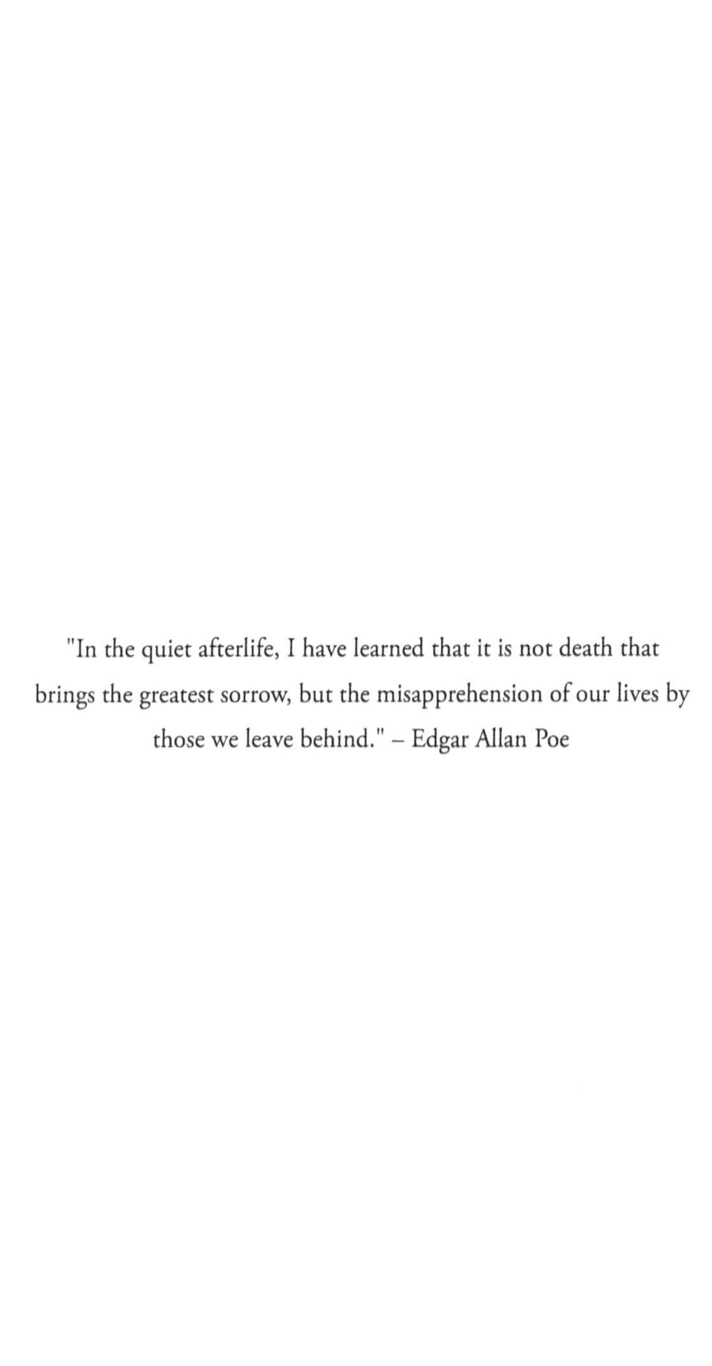

"In the quiet afterlife, I have learned that it is not death that brings the greatest sorrow, but the misapprehension of our lives by those we leave behind." – Edgar Allan Poe

12. Poetry

Has this year started without me ?
As today, it's be a year when we last chat,
We shared our dinner, where laughter once sat
Together we slept, on the single bed, we lay,
But now, in silence, my words convey.

.

Beside her ; i wake by birds' morning song,
In a world where i feels, i don't belong.
Through my routine, i move along,
Yet something feels deeply wrong

.

Down the streets, i walks alone,
Once warm smiles, now turned in stone
At work, whispers follow my path,
In a world where i feel the aftermath.

.

During lunch, i dial with hope,
But silence greets me like a slippery slope.
Returning home, seeks solace there,
But finds emptiness and vacant air.

.

As today, when I walk down the street,
I saw her with someone, my heart skips a beat.

With another man she moved by me while having hand in hand,

It makes my world collapse, like fortress of sand

.

A rush of emotions, a tidal wave inside,

Jealousy sorrow, and wounded pride.

I stands, amidst the crowd,

Feeling small, insignificant, coward and nothing to proud

.

With a heavy heart,I turn away,

Carrying the weight of that fateful day.

Sitting alone in their, once lively space,

A year's absence, a silent race.

.

The date on my phone, a truth untold,

A day isn't pass, but solitude's hold.

Tears fill my eyes as myself finally sees,

Living among memories.

.

In a world where i fade from sight.

I mourn, my heart held tight,

In the days to come, i watch on,

As life moves forward, though I am still gone.

"It seems like this year starts without me,

A world where I can no longer be."

Hearts

"This poem unveils the timeless essence of the human heart, enduring love's joys and sorrows across eras. From ancient times to the present, it remains resilient and wise, a beacon of enduring love wisdom."

Love is the bridge between you and everything

-- Rumi

13. Poetry

Hearts

The saddest thing about love's grand dance,

Is that its beauty fades, and hearts' romance.

Not only love's end brings tears so swift,

But heartbreak too, becomes a forgotten rift.

.

It's amazing how hearts can break,

Yet still, in pieces, love they make.

For every shard and tear that bleeds,

Love persists, in fragile deeds.

.

Hearts will never be practical, we find,

Until they're made unbreakable, designed.

In love's sweet folly, they shatter wide,

Wishing for strength they cannot hide.

.

The hottest love, with passion's fire,

Has the coldest end, a burnt-out pyre.

Love never dies a natural death,

It fades when we forget to give it breath.

.

Yet even as love fades and hearts mend,

We hold its lessons until the end.

cause sadness and joy which love has spun,
Is a journey where two hearts beat as one

.

The saddest truth of love's embrace,
Is knowing it fades, without a trace.
Forever lost, its fleeting grace,
In time's cruel hands, we find our place.

As Grandfather

"In writing this poem, I grapple with the fact that I never truly understood my grandfather's feelings. Instead, I draw upon the lessons he taught me and the qualities I admired in him to paint a picture of his love for my grandmother and his outlook on life. Through my words, I seek to convey his strength of will and his profound impact on me. This poem serves as both a tribute to is memory and a lament for the missed opportunity to say goodbye."

14. Poetry

As Grandfather
How wondrous that day will be,
When on a wheelchair, we sit, you and me,
Waiting for our final breath,
In the stillness of impending death.

.

How strange it seems, yet strangely calm,
As we gaze upon the sky soft and warm
No energy to stand, no will to fly,
Just the quiet whisper of time passing by.

.

Lonely is the weather, devoid of aim,
No future to seek, no one to blame
Only the quiet hum of days gone by,
As we wait for our souls to soar or lie.

.

Terrifying, perhaps, yet oddly serene,
When all purpose fulfilled, all wishes seen,
Sitting with our grandson, a beacon of hope,
That they'll remember our journey, our scope.

.

But if fate should part our hands,
And lead us to distant lands,

You know that I couldn't bear to stay,
If you were to ever go away.

.

So if I should depart before may's end,
Leaving you, my dearest glance
Take care of our grandson, our granddaughter too,
As their last ancestor, it falls to you.

Will you visit my grave, if I fall in duty?

"This poem gives voice to a soldier who prioritized duty above all else, including family and children, and ultimately gave their life in service to their nation. It conveys a heartfelt message from the soldier's grave to their loved one, who faithfully visits as promised, capturing the essence of sacrifice, duty, and enduring love."

"Our dead are never dead to us, until we have forgotten them." - George Eliot

15. Poetry

• 59 •

Will you visit my grave, if I fall in duty?

Now in the heavens, I soar so high
Conversing with the sea, as clouds drift by.
Though my grave lies confined in the earth's embrace
Your presence near it brings a transcendent grace.
From heaven's gates, I feel each breath you take
A divine connection, for both our sakes.

.

When I proposed, I asked with earnest plea
"Will you visit my grave, if I fall in duty?"
You promised, with love unwavering and true
And here you stand, fulfilling what you vowed to do.

.

Though I've relinquished earthly ties and aims
I yearn to know your thoughts, your hopes, your names.
You bear the weight of caring for our children dear
For them, I've secured a safer land and waters clear.

.

I've made this earth a sanctuary, safe and pure
A future bright with love, steadfast and sure.
All I write, all I pen, is a testament to our bond,

Eternal love that stretches far beyond.

.

Your presence stirs my spirit, though I lie below
Your steadfast love and courage, my peace bestow.
From the heavens, I watch over you, ever near
In every whisper of the wind, know I am here.

Again

"This poetry expresses a cycle of emotions we all feel. Within these verses, find echoes of love, loss, and hope. Let each word resonate, stirring your heart and leaving an indelible mark upon your soul."

16. Poetry

Again

I was confined within myself, while you soared the open sky.
Drowning in my pearls of tears, you were the diver passing by.

.

When fate collided our worlds, I fell into a daze,
And when my eyes reopened, I was lost within your gaze.

.

With wings spread wide, together we soared, high above the plain,
It felt as if life's tumultuous boat had found its heaven then.

.

Though prayers werc answered, a poison lingered in my breath,
As autumn's colors faded, our worlds diverged in depth.

.

Now in winter's stormy grip, amidst the relentless rain,
Where have you gone, my love? And where am I again?

Perfect Moments

"In my portrayal of bareness, I aim for casual elegance, capturing the perfect movements witnessed in life. Through vivid descriptions and introspective perspectives, I highlight the inherent perfection within our imperfect world. "

17. Poetry

Perfect Moments

In the realm of perfect sights, behold,
A tree, white and majestic, home to foxes, centuries old.

.

Then, the old man's eyes, weathered and wise,
Witness to seasons, joy, and cries.

.

Then, a bird, resilient, amidst nature's strive,
Crafts its nest after the storm's cruel knife,
Though its eggs are lost, it persists in life.

.

Then, a poor boy's face, innocence in his gaze,
Eating a sandwich amidst life's maze.

.

Then the river's swift and rushing tide,
Stones of myriad hues, side by side.

.

And my faithful dog, companion so true,
From childhood days to nights anew,
Rests on my lap and leaves me when I grew.

A warm good-bye to all my ally

"This poetry conveys the sincerity of emotions that always remain hidden, though the burden on the heart is too much. Despite the weight, these emotions are never conveyed through motions. "

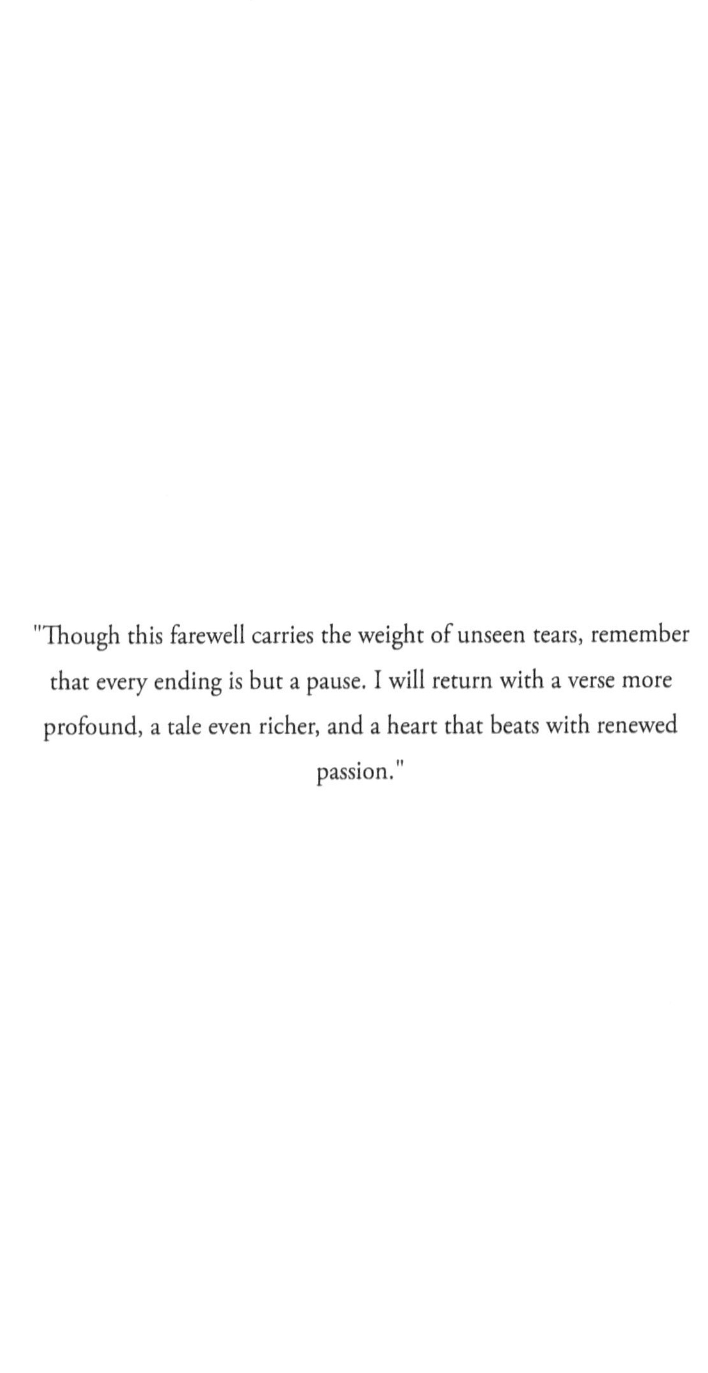

"Though this farewell carries the weight of unseen tears, remember that every ending is but a pause. I will return with a verse more profound, a tale even richer, and a heart that beats with renewed passion."

18. Poetry

A warm Good bye to all my ally

It's a Hard day when i say goodbye
To all my friends and all my Ally

.

In the moments when farewells are said
Emotions swirl, unseen, within my head.
Though friends depart, and alleys fade from view
I stand stoic, with a heart both tired and true.

.

A guy who shuns the tears, I often seem,
Yet beneath the surface, lies a silent stream.
For words may fail, and gestures too obtuse,
To convey the depth of what I can't deduce.

.

But know, within this steadfast, silent guise,
A torrent of feelings, unbidden, flies.
Though I may not praise or shed a tear,
My waves of emotion remain sincere.

.

So as the day bids adieu to light's embrace,
Know within me, a symphony takes place.

For though my outward demeanor may be calm and sun
Thank you, dear friends, for everything you've done,
As we part ways now, our separate paths begun

.

Thanking you for all the laughter and fun
As we dance away, under the setting sun.

19. "Poetry by Friends."

Smile

Smile a gentle curve of joy's embrace in life's vast sea, a tranquil, shining grace.

It speaks of happiness both near and far. A language understood, a shining star.

A flicker of warmth in the darkest nights, a beacon of hope, a source of light, it soothes the wound, calms the troubled soul, a universal language, making whole.

With lips upturned, its levels sweet refrain, A balm for sorrow, a healer of pain, A smile, a treasure, a gift so pure, In its radiant glow, lies all curve.

by Aryan Sharma

Somewhere only we know
The days passed by like a firefly
With colours of leaves changing and barks of trees dry
Some memories drenched us in tears
Some of them gave us laughter and cry
I wonder sometimes how it could really happen
Once we were kids and now we have got no one to pamper
How a memory of tears brings us joy
How a laughing memory makes us cry
We all are getting old with passing time
Without realizing the significance of each moment
Then, there comes a day when we'll be crouched
Unable to standon by own, unable to do anything much
Some of us will be grateful of everything
Some of us will regret of not living
We all lay by ourselves on our sides
Watching the stars of universe dying
Some places will miss us and some will be missed by us
At end we'll take a sip of tea with no retained energy
While on the death bed we significantly lying
Watching the leaves outside drying
With a sweet letter of death in our hands
And scar of past which we all will have
Wtih blurry vision and numb heart beats
We all will want to go somewhere only we know...
By Pratiksha Joshi

Hey There!

Thank you for journeying through this collection of poetry with me. Each poem has been a labor of love, born from moments of inspiration and reflection. Your readership means the world to me, and I value your thoughts and opinions immensely.

If you have any opinions, suggestions, or thoughts about my poetry, please feel free to contact me via email at [akshat.rawaatt@gmail.com or aryansharma6764@gmail.com]. Your feedback is invaluable and will help me grow as a poet.

With heartfelt gratitude,
[AKSHAT RAWAT

ARYAN SHARMA]